TUMOUR

by

Evelyn Lau

OOLICHAN BOOKS
FERNIE, BRITISH COLUMBIA, CANADA
2016

We gratefully acknowledge the financial support of the Canada Council for the Arts, the British Columbia Arts Council through the BC Ministry of Tourism, Culture, and the Arts, and the Government of Canada through the Book Publishing Industry Development Program, for our publishing activities.

Published by
Oolichan Books
P.O. Box 2278
Fernie, British Columbia
Canada V0B 1M0

www.oolichan.com

TUMOUR

As a child he had imagined death as something attacking from outside, but now he knew that it was carried within; we nurse it for years, and it grows.

~ John Updike, "Man and Daughter in the Cold", from The Early Stories 1953-1975.

TABLE OF CONTENTS

PART ONE
ANCIENT HISTORY

PART TWO
TUMOUR

PART ONE

ANCIENT HISTORY

Ancient History

All I wanted was the small grace
of sleep, that swift darkening.
But Ativan led me through the dream gates
to the childhood house on Cambridge Street—
the bang of the metal mailbox,
the lurch of the key in the lock,
the sweaty sheen of linoleum.
Shoes lined against the wall in a mad precision.

My stomach flip-flopped in fear—
somewhere in the house, the mother,
like an escaped tarantula. I am shrieking
in my sleep, a horror film with the sound
turned down, the milk duvet an avalanche
stuffing ears and nostrils with snow,
the scrap-metal sky a dun glow, fading.

Finally, words shatter the surface:
You didn't protect me—
the indignant wail of a four-year-old
choked out in a thick-tongued mumble,
a rasp into the sour breath of the pillow.
Would you believe it?
In a few months I'll be forty.

Alarm

The baby's been kidnapped.
It's not my fault! I scream into the wind
as I run, lugging backpack and diary
past the Korean convenience stores
and Vancouver Specials of my childhood.
The sky the colours of a Ming vase,
goldfish swimming in milk.
But of course it was—
I'd been sneak-eating again,
stealing out to the Super-Valu
for a brick of ice cream and day-old Danish
when the baby needed to be watched,
tended. Was she the sister?
The mother? The endless, intrusive self
psychologists say show up in every dream?

Then the fire alarm went off. 2:45 AM,
red-hot and warbling, ululating
through the building. Doors slamming
along the hall, toilets flushing, fire truck
careening down ashen city streets.
Nervous laughter from the townhouse gardens.
But we'd drown before we roasted—
sprinkler heads like little guardian angels
hovering over us every few feet.
I'm still dressing, moving underwater
slow, when it all dies down—
the alarm sparking in short bursts, fizzing
into uneasy silence. Bird-shaped shadows
on the wall. I've grown too old
for emergencies, real or imagined,
external or self-wrought. Who knew

there'd come a day when the face
in the mirror, the passport photo,
would be this one? In a few hours,
the alarm's miniature twin will blare
the morning news from the bedside table.

Nothing Happened

This was the house on the corner, the one
I passed to and from school each day.
He would have seen me twice
a day, from an upstairs window
or bent over his weeds in the garden—
an ugly girl, clad in scratchy plaid,
moping past. One fist dug deep
into my satchel, searching for day-old
shortbread hidden in a greased bag.
Sweaty bangs, furtive eyes behind
lenses thick as goggles—
some adults said I was shy.
She's sly, my mother declared, *up to no good.*
She won't look me in the eye, a teacher complained,
and my father whipped round in his seat
at the parent-teacher conference:
What's wrong with you?
What are you trying to hide?

One afternoon, the man asked me in—
past the stone lions, pots of lavender,
into the tiled foyer. The tiles were painted
with lemons, oranges, clusters of olives.
Nothing happened. Or something did—
the threat of something, creeping in the air
between us. It thickened my throat,
stuffed my sinuses like pollen.
He fetched his violin, this old man
with his nut-brown bald head,
played it for me like a suitor
in a sunny square, slicing note
after note into the air. His hand on my knee,

a shy spider. (Am I making this up now,
digging diligently as an archeologist,
searching for where it all went wrong?)

But nothing happened. Dust in the corners,
a brass umbrella stand, the bulky Nikes
belonging to his teenage grandsons. .
The bow sawing the violin,
horsehair fraying.
The air so thick it seemed fibrous,
knotting around me like a mesh net,
like pantyhose yanked over the face.
His dark thoughts pouring into me
like motor oil. Maybe I wanted something
to happen, anything at all—
a way out, even this way.

But then he opened the front door.

Something Happened

Chinatown. Stacks of oranges for sale,
globes of citrus fruit heaped into a gold mountain,
gleaming in the midday sun. My parents jockeying
for position amid the chaos of bargain-seekers,
the slap and jostle of elbows and shopping bags—
snatching produce from this mound of plenitude,
a flood of fruit for pennies a pound.
The wonder of living in a land
like Canada, where there was so much food
you could let it go to waste—
toss out a mouldy bean or wilted lettuce,
scrape into the garbage the last cold grains
of rice from your bowl. My father had driven miles
out of the way for this sale and he was smiling
with relief, blinking the perpetual haze
of worry from his eyes—

yes, here even the unemployed could eat,
there would be no digging through the dirt
for roots and worms. My mother's hands darted
through the pile, squeezing, juggling,
hefting an orb to her face for a sniff
of distant Florida sunshine, yards of citrus trees
where fruit nestled among the shiny leaves
like gems. Her fingertips read the Braille
of dimples and soft spots like fontanelles
in the rind, searching for signs of rot—
dots of green and white blight,
the sunken squish of a bruise
that meant spoiled flesh.

I hovered on the edge of the crowd,
the shrivelled po-pos who had known starvation
shoving me aside on their way in. Bored,
embarrassed as any ten year old by this display
of need, yearning to go home to *Gone With the Wind*—
I fantasized myself a budding Scarlett O'Hara
in the skirt of stiff fabric I was wearing
for the first time that day,
powder blue, with the sheen and slipperiness
of polyester. I was jiggling
with impatience, pent up life.

That's when the man came around the corner.
A burnt gargoyle of a face,
drunk at noon, a bum from nearby skid row—
his first grab was sly, furtive,
but when I stood mute and motionless
as someone playing statue,
his lips stretched in a rictus of pleasure
and he came around again, and again,
circling the block, thrusting his hand
under my skirt while a few feet away
my parents picked oranges. Was that all?
A sale on oranges in Chinatown,
my father out of work and worried,
a man's grimy hand between my legs. How proud
and grown-up I felt in this hold of silence,
guarding my parents' little kingdom,
keeping them safe in the discount supermarket.

Burns

I don't remember the injury.
The pot of roiling water knocked off
the element, the cascade of scorching drops
splashing slow-motion through the frozen air.
I didn't see her there, she'd say afterwards,
again and again, her face abashed
and lit with love. I imagine her horror
when it happened, the sound of her shriek,
the rush to embrace and inspect for damage.
The avalanche of her relief
when I stood there, whole, spotted
like a leopard but unharmed, too surprised
to wail. The pain, what there was
of it, too foreign for my soft, still-forming
mind to grasp. Probably it had been my fault—
lurking around her legs in the kitchen
like a neighbourhood cat, rubbing up
against her good smell of talcum powder
and rhubarb pie. I remember the afterwards,
how she handled me with such care
for days. As though I was newborn
again, unbroken by the rough passage.
Almost reverent in my presence, her slim
pale hands rubbing ointment in circles
onto my body like a blessing.

A decade later, her own arms would be scarred
with burns like a chef's, from the hours
of angry labour in the kitchen—
the slamming of hot wok onto the stove,
the splash-back of spitting corn oil.
Spoons and knives hurled into the sink,

cutting board slapped onto the counter.
A cacophony of pots and pans yanked
from cupboards, the crackle of sizzling
stir-fry like flames in hell—
beneath it all the ballad of her frustrations,
a spoken-word diatribe accompanied
by kitchen implements.

Motion Sickness

It's here again—that tilt
when I turn my head, a sensation
of slippage, trees and clouds and mountains
liquefying, as if someone's taken their thumb
and smeared the still-wet images
on a Polaroid. The world's gone streaky,
like the day on the ferry when the wood grain
of the sill began to flow like a river
of porridge, and the floor poured
back and forth, and I cried
into my hands remembering
my mother on the ferry thirty years ago—

her white ghost-face, jaws clenched
against nausea. Her rage at my father
for taking my hand in his and steering me
into the gift shop, where no treat
was forbidden. A rainbow panorama
of sweets, like fairy food
sprinkled from heaven! I chose Smarties,
rattling inside their neat cardboard box,
darling discs, candy shell crunch
and cores of chocolate—

like dropping buttons onto your tongue,
their pleasing pebble shapes so slick
and soothing. I bit and sucked,
savouring the crimson and lavender
and tangerine dyes, leaving one
so long on my tongue it resembled
a bleached stone you'd find on the shore. . .

I was returning to show her,
to stick out my tongue spackled
with sugar shards and blur of melted cocoa.
It never occurred to me she might be jealous.
Where was her treat, her spoonful
of sweetness, when every day was self-
sacrifice? The hate in her face
slammed into us like a wave
cresting the deck, obscuring the sky's
blue glimmer, the islands sliding by.

Janny

I remember my cousin Janny
hunched over the kitchen sink,
scrubbing the household dishes at dawn
that summer we visited Grandma
in California. Treated like a slave
in feudal China, brunt of Grandma's wrath—
piece of trash, monkey on her back,
good-for-nothing bastard daughter
of her own fourth child, Auntie No. 4
who had Janny out of wedlock—

still a shocker for a Chinese family
in the '70s. It was rumoured
my aunt never knew the father, or that
he rightly washed his hands of her,
this tired baggy-eyed woman
who trudged home from work
at the fast food restaurant, reeking
of grease, ripping the brown-and-yellow
paper hat off her head as she sat down
to dinner in her stained uniform.
Auntie No. 4, who decades later would die
in a homeless shelter for battered women . . .

Janny barely spoke during our visit—
scrawny-shouldered, shaking
with shyness, beaten down by the daily
hail of Grandma's hatred. I remember
the way she flinched at loud noises
or sudden movements, with a look
of such tense, whimpering terror in her eyes
it made you want to hit her—

yet somehow she escaped. The news
of her life filtered through to me, over the years:
Your cousin Janny's going to school.
Janny's getting married, moving to Texas.
Janny has children now.
How? I always wondered. It was a puzzle,
the laws of the universe upended,
the sky swimming with fish and the sea
crammed with clouds. Maybe
there was an escape route, a hidden exit,
a trap door I hadn't found in all
these years of wild searching.
Maybe my cousin had stumbled upon it
in her despair, crawled her way out
into a normal life. I pictured her
in some sun-soaked small town—
white picket fence, toys in the yard—
waving to her kids on the schoolbus,
folding herself into the tanned arms
of a man who loved her.

The call came this weekend:
Your cousin Janny passed away.
She killed herself. Her 15-year-old son
(a straight-A student, my aunt hastened
to add) came home from class to find her
overdosed on the living room sofa.
I thought she had escaped
her fate, and maybe there were days
she thought so too, living out a normal life
like someone else's dream.
Living a life like it was rightfully hers.

The Shrine

My grandfather, three decades dead,
speaks to me from inside the picture frame;
or tries to, there's no words, just lips
bared over teeth, the grin
of a man being sliced open
without anaesthetic. His photograph

still stands in the shrine
at the back of your house,
behind the bowl of wrinkled oranges,
under the Chinese character shaped
like a pagoda, hammered in gold.

His name was Pak Wo, and you say
it was a curse from birth, that he carried
misery on his back like a donkey—
twelve hungry mouths
and a raging wife waiting for him
at the threshold of his apartment
after days spent hawking fountain pens.

In my memory he is black and white
like a photograph from another century.
Wears a wool suit, wire-framed glasses.
He smells of ink and camphor,
chrysanthemum tea and a battered
steamer trunk that made the voyage
overseas from China. Now his grandchildren,

my cousins, are scattered across North America.
The dutiful ones are church-going,
married, or in university

earning degrees in law, engineering
and pharmacy. One committed suicide
this year, swallowing pill after pill
until the lovely chill unfolded like a flower
through her limbs in the Texas heat.

Some days I know I'm losing
my way, and Grandfather's the one
I want to interrogate. I want to hear
the whole story, to trace the poison
back to its source, the blot of black ink
curdling in my veins. Last night I dreamt

of a storm. Snow poured from the milk sky.
I shuffled in plastic slippers,
the heels peeling away.
In one hand I carried a live chicken,
its bony feet hooked between my fingers,
a gift for Pak Wo and his starving family.

Thawed

During this winter's flu, it was Fiona,
daughter of my former doctor, who brought
chicken soup. Organic, assembled
by her hands, snatched from the freezer
just before the poetry reading
and tucked inside an Eddie Bauer bag.
A day later, it was still half-frozen—
I hefted it in my hands, the jar glazed
with hoarfrost, shook it
but it didn't make a sound—
its contents creamy as pig fat,
speckled with spice, a salty trifle
wobbling atop a murky, sandy crust.

I wrenched the lid and an odd slurry
slid into the pot, a miniature aquarium
blooming with Arctic ice flowers, snow crystals
hazing the surface, a strange sorbet
with jellied layers. I have to say,
it didn't look promising.
Reminded me of the foul soups my mother
made to cure colds, as if indulgence
had cracked the door open to disease,
and only bitterness would seal it shut.
I fished a string of chicken skin,
grey and tentacular, out of the depths;
shrugged, plopped it back in.
Scraped it all in and waited.

The sludge melted down to a gold broth
that I sipped, and then guzzled,
startled out of semi-delirium,

ambushed by deliciousness.
A lifetime of feasts and flavours,
and it seemed this was the first thing
I'd tasted, straining it impatiently
between my teeth when I wanted to suck
and gulp, tongue the grooves
of the clay mug, rescue the recycled
jar from the trash to shake out
any wasted drops, sediment.
An orchestra of herbs hummed
on my palate. I didn't know my own greed
until a blister the circumference
of the roof of my mouth began to form,
a bubble of broth billowing
like a tiny hot air balloon. Then it burst
and I swallowed a swell of salt,
hoping for a final trace
of Fiona's homemade chicken soup.

Sunday at Kate's

We spurned Copper Moon, gulped Naked Grape.
Ate Raincoast Crisps like crunching into cedar.

This was the long decade of olives and hummus
at every party. Our neighbours were at the parade

and we were at Kate's, listening to poetry.
I was admiring Daniela's red jeggings

and missed the reader's reference
to ancient Greek mythology.

Two eagles circled overhead and Kate said,
Oh, those are PK's eagles—

years of living by the sea and the day
they visited was the day PK Page died.

We remembered her lovely legs,
her embroidered shawl.

Russell fell off a ladder yesterday
but didn't have anything stronger than Tylenol.

There was no longer any upside to pain—
had it ever been worth it? Of course,

the inspiration. The spark of creation!
I made a lame joke about our lives

going downhill and Catherine turned
in a fury, and I could see how things could sour

in a hurry. How brittle the scratched surface,
how permeable. What had we become?

The sort of people who discuss the price
of real estate at poetry readings.

Soon another tower would twist
outside Kate's window, halving the light.

The ocean was temporary, the sky.
Calvin said, *Look, there's still spots*

of colour in the winter landscape.
The yellow twigs in the dead balcony garden.

The pebbles nested on the white
windowsill were blue.

Fogged

For weeks we lived inside a cloud.
Glimpses of orange leaves,
mohair sweaters, church windows.
The news broadcast million-dollar sunsets
above the fog, enjoyed by the owners
of glass houses along the Sea-to-Sky,
who hauled Italian marble and slabs
of stainless steel to their dream homes
on the cliffs. What did we work for?
That weekend the poets ascended
to the village above the cloud,
among Japanese tourists and turning maples,
near Lost Lake and River of Broken Dreams.
We drank pinot grigio and ate prosciutto-
wrapped melon in the five-star hotel;
it's just how you'd imagine poets live,
in deluxe corner suites overlooking
a steamy hot tub, green ski run,
stand of trees doing their slow burn.
That weekend a motorcyclist died
on his way to Whistler, buried
under a barrage of logs
that tumbled off a truck as it slid
and slammed onto its side.
We could agree, we were lucky.
Here the sun shone, though not
in the windowless conference room.
Here we spoke in turn, bespectacled,
buttoned up like academics—
not like poets of previous generations,
fists flying and bottles breaking,
or was that ever true?

Everyone was kind, everyone was gracious.
Sunday we drove home past eagles
and golf courses, mountain run-off
the colour of absinthe. The cloud below
smothered the city, still there.

The Condo Down the Street

Pot lights like pale moons, in the scraped ceiling.
Pendant lamps gilding the granite island,
suspended on cables thin as spider thread.
All the appliances Miele—
the induction oven, roiling the pan

of water to a boil in seconds; the washer,
cradling its load of clothes as carefully as a pair
of human hands—stainless steel with the sheen
of platinum. Each high-gloss drawer soft-close
so as not to disturb the hush of money.

How much better to be a monk
without desire, in a cell with a cot
and a cold floor! Not a calorie of thought
wasted on what or what not to wear—
the same saffron robe, bare feet,
battered begging bowl extended
for the day's feast or famine.

Yet I am sick with desire
for subway tiles and marble floors,
silk rugs and custom closets,
a home office with not a fingerprint
or ink smudge in sight. All of it bright-white,
as if nothing had to be done for money.

So who has the richer life? the doctor asks.
A poet, and all I ever wanted was money.

Dear Doctor

In dreams, it takes all night to reach you—
blind driving down unfamiliar roads,
twisty mountain passes, suburban cul-de-sacs
not on any map. Then at last,

the mirrors in the green stairwell.
The mirrors so close to the entrance
I could have walked straight into myself.
For years, this was the shape of the world.

The plain room and its myriad dimensions,
radiating outward like meaning
from the bound lines of a poem—
the meaning in the space, the breath.

The silence. Clouds of curry rising
from the Indian restaurant below,
the shuffle of mail through your meaty hands,
the worn patch on the seat of the leather armchair,

duct-taped together. Last night I dreamt
I rode a boat through choppy water to see you.
You lived on a high cliff above wintry seas.
It was a paradise of pastoral beauty,

drenched in the syrupy light of summer.
Cottages with paned windows,
gardens overgrown with roses, wildflowers.
Bees bumbling through brambles,

furry as tiny bears, freighted with honey.
Butterflies like lofted petals
tearing through the sappy air.
How I longed to live there too!

Only the ocean lay between us.

Window View, Spring

The trees screening my room
from the street are in bloom again,
scribbled with green. Broken crockery
in the soil, the ragged paint daubs
of daffodils. Cherry blossoms
clogging the gutters.

Twenty years I've been eyeing
this shrub outside my window,
watching it grow an inch a year,
its branches candled with cones.
Where does anyone go from here?

Today two workmen levitating
in a crane above the downtown street
removed the hands from the clock face
above the intersection. Now the gold circle
is complete, hovering like a harvest moon
above the tower called Eden.

The hours evaporate, the thawed days.
Seagulls sail past the highrises,
ancient as pterodactyls.
The old crows watch from the wires—

Good-bye, Santa Monica

The horizon's gone, buried beneath a froth
of smog, flat blank glare. At the end of the pier,
bobbing sailboats and veer of vertigo—
the measureless water, seesaw of wavelets,
tilt and tug of the tide.
You thought you would have landed here
long ago, lived as if inside a movie—
caged in glass and polished concrete,
one wall a blue ocean. Blood orange sunset
drizzled in a line across the sky.
Now you are middle-aged, repentant
most days, lost among the advancing
young on the Third St. Promenade,
their tidal beauty sweeping you aside.
Say good-bye to houses the size of plantations,
the Ferris wheel and the fortune teller,
this life you swore would be yours
two decades ago in a motel on Ocean,
a tiny surfer tangled in the waves
through the speckled window.
Good-bye to the fringe of palm trees,
birds of paradise with exploded beaks.
Good-bye to the homeless population
stretching and scratching on their benches
at dawn, muttering prayers or incantations
over their midday meals, swaddled in terrycloth
like housewives. Good-bye to the Big Blue Bus,
the Bible-thumper reminding you of your sins;
the copper man with snakes strangling his arms,
the girl with nothing but her guitar. This room
without a view, facing away from the Pacific.
At last you are here, at the end

of the pier, cradled by water and tired flesh
and bone, seasick, looking for land.

California Beach Town

Water as blue as a blue raspberry Slurpee!
Porpoises torquing in the waves,
a pelican waddling down the dock.
Volleyball posts inked "The Office"
and "The School". Summer rentals

on the side streets, lanes lined
with cactus gardens and palms,
coconut clouds of spray-on
sunscreen. Feet on furniture.
Heaven a white Cape Cod cottage

on a Crystal Pier, the washing machine
toss and thump of the surf
under the bed. Snort of sea lions.
On your left, pastel bicycles
whizzing past. Sunburned flesh

pumped up and greased for the grill,
sizzling under the sun's heat lamp
in the diffuse sky. You'll dream
of this life as if it were yours—
ogle real estate, settle for road trips.

Meanwhile, the shacks on the wharf—
crammed with floral bikinis, rainbow leis,
plumeria hairclips pressed from Styrofoam—
let the Californians imagine
they're in Hawaii.

Futile

At the dinner party the conversation
went on and on. Over green mash
of guacamole, shards of tortilla chips,
vegan brownies from the organic market.

Sun and stars winking in the bathroom,
terracotta tile underfoot like red earth,
lumps of rock and shell harvested
from some distant, protected beach.

Everyone had the flu, everyone got better.
No one died, except Flora,
the neighbourhood crank,
who was 92 and a racist, actually.

Laminate plank glowing in the corona
cast by the fire log firelight.
Stainless steel like a silver
second skin. The pornographic protrusions
of drawer pulls. Our dream homes

were swept away by hurricanes, tsunamis,
debt and foreclosure, by too many
trips to the mall and a weakness
for overpriced treats
to get through the day. Meanwhile

that cabin on the beach just floated away.
We make do with the space we have.
The roller shades made me feel rich,
the treaded carpet poor.
The trips to Home Depot made me feel insane.

You said you visited ten tile stores
to find the right flooring, vowed to open
a tile store and call it "Futile".
We laughed and laughed
and fondled the renovations.

Remembrance Day

On the eleventh hour of 11/11/11,
I am at Winners with the other bargain hunters,
the early Christmas shoppers, the bored.
It's soggy, miserable out. The sky
has swallowed all the light, sunk
into a greyed puff of dirty down.
Trenches of rainwater in the road,
burnt leaves mulching underfoot,
mourning of seagulls. A clerk's voice
breaks into the piped-in '80s music
to remind us of the day. She stumbles
over a few lines of "Flanders Fields",
announces a minute of silence.
Who knew sixty seconds could be
this long? We rotate round the racks
of marked-down designer clothes
in the uncomfortable stillness.
I glance around—there's nothing
on anyone's face, just a slight frown
of concentration as a sweater slips
off a hanger, a flinch of irritation
at being bumped by a stranger's cart
from behind. My friend Szeming
who was ten years old during the Japanese
occupation of Hong Kong remembers
the meagre two meals a day, going without
the luxury of socks or sweets. Remembers
the crowd peering into a bucket
on the sidewalk—a street urchin's head,
discarded after the rest of him
had been used for food. The relentless rain
drills the windows. In the distance,

the jet roar of thunder. What a relief
to be inside this bunker, bathed
in artificial heat and light, training our sights
on the perfect winter coat, holiday dress.
Finally, the tinny music cranks up again
and we relax, relieved of the burden
of remembering. Some young woman
is singing about love, how love
is like a battlefield.

Hong Kong

On Lamma Island you were full of yellow wine.
At dinner, a tipsy poet proposed marriage
when you said, *I'm good with money—*
years of poverty had made you frugal, a trait
more desirable finally than looks or charm.
Cockroaches skittered along the dock,
between the tanks of dying fish.
He forgot his own wife was younger
than you, that he already had
what others wanted. You felt visible again,
the night edged with risk.
Somewhere out there were opium dens,
dragons, the bloated hulls of yachts
at the Aberdeen Marina.
This was almost the city of your birth.
Refrigerated shopping malls
with luxury goods and skin-lightening creams,
butchers' alleys where blood
and meat juice sluiced into the gutters.

Returning, the junk stalled in the sea.
Blue and emerald shapes of land
loomed out of the black-silk night.
The quiet. Suddenly you wanted to cry,
thinking of the toy sailboats
motoring the pond in Victoria Park,
caged birds chirping among the palms.
The library where your father studied
as a young man, climbing the stone steps
with his satchel of engineering books,
numbers crowding his head
the way words would crowd yours

all your life. The ghost of your dead aunt
rushing into traffic, double-decker buses
and blaring cars, hurrying for home.

Past Life

For years you've had the same vision,
or hallucination, an image that shivers
across the screen of your eyelids
in the patchwork fragments before sleep—

a woman in the charred stairwell
of an opium den, swathed in scarlet silk,
her skin desiccated, mottled mahogany
stretched over skeleton. Inside, men adrift

on the carved beds. Was this your past life,
a pulse of sense-memory emerging
in the porous seconds before the erasure
of sleeping-pill sleep? Once, in Hong Kong,
rifling through a rack of cards at Dymocks,

your fingers froze on the bleached print
of a room with bamboo walls,
lantern-hung ceiling, emaciated men
sprawled on daybeds with their pipes
and powders, gesturing at mirages

in the smoke-swirled air. It was like stumbling
on a photo of your childhood home.
Here, the passing of the hours
is marked by the dry-swallow of pills,
then the triumph of collapsing

on the daybed, the sky the tropical
swimming-pool green of a California
sky at night, droning with helicopters.
The codeine crumbles inside you,

its opiate grains sugaring your bloodstream,
and then you are there—

the doorway, the swaddled woman,
the descent which is like a rising,
your breath blooming in your chest
like the work of meditation. The lotus
and the mountain monastery.

The glimpse of the river of gold.

Game Two, Stanley Cup Playoffs 2011
(as experienced from a VSO concert at the Orpheum Theatre)

We can hear them behind the violins,
behind the harp, the mezzo-soprano in her peacock dress—
the mob outside the Orpheum, swarming the gates.
The orchestra plays on, as if this gilded cavern
were a ship sailing into an iceberg,
plummeting into the parting ocean
of permanent dark. Mahler wrote his *Songs
of the Earth* the year his daughter died
of scarlet fever and diphtheria, the year the doctor
handed him his own death-diagnosis.
What is there to do, he laments,
echoing Li Bai in his centuries-old despair,
what is there to do but drink
and drink some more, to survive
this intolerable existence? Outside
these golden walls, the mob roars
its intolerable joy, its thunderous ovation.
When it's over, we stumble
onto streets paved with smithereens
of glass. Faces leer at us from the darkness,
ablaze with alcohol. The scarlet aria
of sirens, a symphony of car horns—
this frenzy further evidence, you say,
of a dying culture. Are we so near
the end? Tomorrow morning we will see
what they did in their unbearable happiness—
mailboxes toppled on their sides,
branches ripped off sap-bleeding trees,
cyclamen and petunia stomped into the crushed earth.

Gratitude

It's too, too, too beautiful.—Jun Lin's last Facebook post,
accompanying a photograph of a park, days before he was
murdered, and his body dismembered, allegedly by Luka
Magnotta

We don't yet know how it began.
Perhaps he posed as a potential friend,
inviting you for Starbucks and biscotti
after class, or Labatts and chicken wings
on the weekend, hockey on TV.
Perhaps you looked forward to the visit,
bounding up the stairs bearing some small gift
like a good guest, some small token
to appease the gods of hospitality
at the front door. That was
the sort of man you were—
showing up for work at the grocery store
on time every day, hoping to find in Canada
not money or status, like your classmates,
but love. A romantic. This painful light

shines in your face in photographs,
moon-bright, a little shy, eager
to please. An A student, studying computers
and engineering, a decade older
than your classmates, old enough that in China,
you wrote, they would respectfully
call you "uncle"—
what you wanted were peers.
Friends, lovers. You were lonely,
vulnerable in your loneliness.
Wanted someone to ride with you

on the midnight subway train in Montreal,
its flickering hospital-green half-light
you captured on film, deserted snowscapes
you posted to friends in China—
you the only figure in all that ground.

But then there was that day in the park.
It was *too, too, too beautiful*—
a park others rushed through every day,
heads bowed over texts and tweets
while you stood gaping in awe, in a daze
of wonder, craning your neck
to see the sky swimming with green,
the drowsy parasols of the maples
sprinkling your delighted face
with sap, silent gust of wind swelling

through the stately willows, the vegetable whiff
of mown grass, *too much*, you thought,
it's too much, days before it was taken
from you in a blaze of rage. Montreal,
released from the frozen grip of winter,
leafing out in the spring.
You had worked and saved,
worked and saved for years
to arrive at this place.

The Chinese Museum

Grace committed suicide again, you say
in your second language, rather than *attempted*,
as if my aunt were doomed to an endless cycle
of reincarnated lives to end. We're walking
in the Chinese museum, down a corridor
of black and white photographs—
six immigrant bachelors sharing one
housekeeping room, crammed
like mackerel in the hold of a ship.

We're admiring the artefacts—
abacuses strung with jet stones,
cotton robes with cloud-shaped collars,
the opium bed whose lacquered rose-carved sides
could hold a man safe inside his dream
all day, like an infant in a barred crib.

How small our ancestors were, last century—
the merchant families posing for photos
in their stiff, gilded clothes;
the men who left wives and babies behind
to work on the rails and in the mines;
the ones who hung themselves in their single rooms
to escape gambling debts, drug addiction,
to escape their lives.

Grace, Auntie No. 12, was fished out
of the sea into which she leapt,
days after she'd gone missing again.
The seams of her clothes were seeded
with sand, so you knew where she'd been—
at the beach, watching the waves for days.

We hug good-bye, I hurry through Chinatown—
past shivering clerks in souvenir stores,
surviving beneath brass Buddhas and bamboo fans,
paper lanterns and polyester kimonos.
Home is a one-bedroom, above an alley.
After twenty years of living here, it took a friend
to point out that the view from my window—
moss-covered rocks on a rooftop—
wasn't just moss and rocks, but a rock garden.

PART TWO

TUMOUR

Tumour

The surgeon cracked open your skull,
eyeballed the tumour and its tentacles,
closed you back up like a gift he meant to return.
It was the size of a walnut, and malignant.
You hugged him when you woke, thought
he'd saved your life.

She still recognizes people, your sister wrote.
She has a good appetite—
she eats and eats. I think
she is just like a baby now.

*

You were there in the time
before memory, when I was a baby
on the potty, greedy for kisses
and sticky handfuls of penny candy.
You wanted me more than any man
has ever wanted me—

so of course I had to escape
your childless clutches, rebuff such smothering love.
We hadn't spoken in six years—
six years of cards and letters scanned
then crammed into desk drawers
or wastebaskets, six years of pleas
and enticements: *Niece, I bought a gift for you,*
don't make me return it . . .

Once you snuck past the front gate
of the condo complex, planted yourself

outside my door, knocked and knocked.
I waited on the other side, breath held,
heat filling my face. Knocked and knocked,
until you went away, footsteps fading
down the wallpapered hall.

*

I remember your wedding, and climbing stairs
to the gilded stage for photographs.
The sea of red in the Chinese restaurant,
the dumplings in sweet soup for dessert.
The scratch of my starched dress. Your hot,
hopeful face turned towards the bursting light.

Your broad face brimmed with disappointment
all those times I left you, in restaurants
or at bus stops, as I hurried back
to my busy young life. The bus transfer
in your fist, the polyester pants that flapped
around your ankles as you continued
on our journey, alone.

*

I brought chrysanthemums to the hospital.
Thought them cheerful, a giant pot
of gold, a cauldron of sunshine.
A peace offering? You gave them a glance,
waved them away—
Put them over there, you said, and then I saw
the rows of chrysanthemums on the sill,
flowers for the dying. Ugly as macrame.

Should have bought the sunflower,
craning its face to the light. But I imagined it
dying in a matter of days—
the drooping stalk, the crimped
and browning petals. How mournful
you might be when it was gone.

*

Such a gracious space, this final terminal—
crowded with flowers, lit with art,
dream-catchers swinging in the windows.
Books bricking a bronze fireplace.

Your hair strewn with grey, mouth agape
with missing teeth you were too frugal to fix.
The jagged scar crazing your forehead,
the bloody scratches on your legs
as though you'd crawled through barbed wire,
trying to escape.

*

For weeks I sat by your hospital bed—
that was a lie. More like an hour here
or there, before fleeing into the sterile
corridors, out the sliding glass doors,
gasping for green air. Getting away
from the tremor in your papery hands,
the confusion stuttering your speech.

You lunged for the receiver,
but the telephone hadn't rung.
You were ready for breakfast,
but it was seven in the evening.

The world was tilting on its axis,
everything familiar and stable
slipping and sliding into the sea.

*

Regrets? There was the dune buggy ride
you wished you'd taken in Oregon,
on that cratered landscape that
mimicked the surface of the moon—
sand from the dunes spilt
across the highway, sea grass
surging in the wind. And the surf
that sounded just like the conch
you kept on the sill—

in that house I spent so many
childhood afternoons, sticky fingers
squeezing and probing your souvenirs.
The fake bear rug splayed in front
of the fireplace, the gourd with its belly
rattling with dried seeds, that shell.
I pressed it to my ear and heard the roar
of my future life rushing towards me.

*

Days of sunshine, wheeling
into fall. I fed you squares of chocolate,
brown saliva dribbling down your chin
like shit. Plastic sheet on the bed,
creams for diaper rash on the nightstand.
At your neglected house, ants
swarmed the foyer, weeds peered into the window.

When your shirt came unbuttoned
I saw the puff of your belly, the sag of your breasts.
In their plastic slippers your feet were gross
swollen boats, dappled with burgundy,
the toenails coal-black.
Eyes blank as plum pits, stones.

*

Nothing stayed the same, but it didn't get better.
The tumour grew and grew, defeating the Decadron.
Dinner thinned to liquids—
broccoli soup, tea, gelatin.

The ward sank into darkness
as the days grew shorter—
nurses' feet padding up and down the halls,
ping of bells rung by patients needing attention,
whispers and groans. The beds that filled,
then emptied. A stranger in the elevator,
sobbing harshly next to me.

*

Your hand smooth and dry in mine,
your grip adhesive as an infant's.
One dark eye opening to look at me
from the bottom of the well, wave after wave
of sickness washing over you. Opening, closing,
your hand squeezing—

and then not. Now liquids made you choke.
Dinner was a spoonful of thickened peach juice.
I pushed a swab around your mouth,
clumsily, as though driving a tractor. The nurses came

to turn you, they ran their hands over you—
Oh, she's still warm, they said in surprise—

but your face was cool, cooling.
It's winter. A cruise ship with its myriad
lighted windows sailed out into the bay,
heading for the glaciers.

Life on Mars

Somehow, a decade after her death,
he's still alive, locked inside
the crumbling house. His teeth

have eroded to dark sand in his mouth,
to soil. He doesn't bathe
or go outside for weeks at a time,

though every few days he'll collect
papers off the stoop—
Does that count?

The carpet crunches under my feet
like a rocky beach, strewn with discard.
Windows shut for so long

the latches have fused to the frame.
Towers of magazines toppled
on their sides like blasted buildings;

a snow-bank of unopened mail
on the gouged mattress. This is the week
Rover "Curiosity" sends back

snapshops from Mars, grainy views
of rock and desert not so different
from a gravel pit or excavation site.

My uncle was a physicist, navigating
the canyons and mountain passes
of his deep thoughts, following

glimmering trails of inspiration
into the darkness. We twitch
the rabbit ears on his TV,

marvel at the ordinary images,
argue about the failure of Biosphere 2—
I thought the scientists couldn't get along.

No, he says, *it was lack of oxygen.*
As soon as they sealed that place
shut, they were doomed.

The Day I Died

I remember the muddy light
through the tacked-up curtains.
The sour smell of the stranger's
rainbow afghan, knit bedspread
draped over the mattress like a cobweb.
His dark penis swinging between his legs.

My wobbly face in the watermarked mirror.
The bruise-coloured body I lowered
into the porcelain bath
wasn't mine any longer.
It looked like a field of blue flowers.

The rattle of the pills as they skittered
into the sink, their vinegar taste
going down. The half-rotten stew
he cooked all day on the wood stove,
adding to it hour
after hour, the stew we sopped up
with expired sourdough, lurched
into the back of my throat.

I was 14. Like most suicides,
woke up a few hours later
in semi-darkness. Grey veils
of rain through the evergreens,
the glimmer of light on water.
The sizzle and stench of burning
wood in my pores.

Strange, how sometimes now
it's not that day that seems unreal,

but all the years since then—
a hallucination, a trick
of dying brain cells firing,
misfiring, someone else's
half-glimpsed life, halfway gone.

Face

A writer once said, *Face it,*
no one's ever going to give you a second glance.

A judge once wrote,
Your face is like a lotus blossom,
your lips like an exotic orchid.

You live in every reflective surface,
snag my gaze in a shop window,
a polished picture frame, a teaspoon.
I must see you twenty times a day, yet somehow
I missed the moment you came unpinned
from the framework of bones that stretched you
taut like a canvas, and slid—

settling into your current motley state
of pouches and hollows, as if invisible fingers
had prodded and pulled at the flesh,
scattered sunspots across your cheeks
and chin, pawed the skin around your eyes,
pinched a tag or mole out of pure malice.
White hairs zigzag from your temples,
streak the childish fringe you've maintained
since your first haircut, as though
this could keep you a child.

Yet there are days you still surprise me,
seen from an angle in flattering sunset light—
times I would secretly agree with the judge's verdict,
glance around for confirmation
and realize no one's looking.

Skin

You came into this world a sheet of blank paper,
fresh linen, a bowl of almond milk.
My life has left its marks on you—
the puckering of scars, railroad tracks
of stitches, the needle pricks
and tick-tack-toe forearms
of a wayward adolescence.
Your keloid tissue shines silvery
as snail slime, meandering
down the scratching posts of my limbs.

Now I am in preservation mode—
moisturize after every shower,
stay out of the sun, avoid parabens
and parfums, leaf through magazines
in search of the latest miracle cream,
functional food, do everything
to prolong youth. To give you
that *satin texture*, that *radiant glow*.
Line the pockets of Estee Lauder,
the dermatologists at Clinique, even when
there's no money for the mortgage.

These days, you don't need a punched window
or a razor blade to register damage—
a mosquito bite, a scratched hive
will leave a stain that takes six months to fade.

Brain

There might be something wrong with you.
Or is it all in your head?

Migraines flash across your landscape
like electrical storms, scorching trees and shrubs.
Anxiety torches your neuron pathways,
obliterating names, faces, human language.
You stare at a line of poetry for hours
before stuttering to a stop
like a seized-up computer.
You search so ardently for the right word
you implode in a shower of sparks
and scrolling numerals. Some days
you are shrouded in fog like a coastline—
a horror-movie fog that creeps in
like poison gas, like lethargy.
Other days you are on fire—
when I touch my forehead, my fingertips
leap away singed—
I can almost smell you burning,
a tofu scramble left on high heat on the stove,
swelling against the stricture of the skull.

The middle of the night is your favourite time—
you replay reel after reel of embarrassments,
spark lame conversations with a Round Table wit
that evaporates in the morning light.

Gallbladder

Who knew you were even there?
Tucked under the liver, a shrivelled
and sunken pear, small sac, treasure bag
of stones, a stitch in my side—
you are chewing me up from the inside,
your constant gnawing, your spastic contortions
bruising the liver, sending its gamma readings soaring.
When you attack, women say
it's like childbirth, without the happy ending.

You wake me in the night, announce yourself
just under the ribcage, to the right,
you who slept so soundly for decades,
pink and plump, now fiercely awake
and complaining, mottled black
and diseased. I've fed you a rich diet
of sugar and fat, groomed myself into
alliteration, the typical gallbladder patient—
a fat, fertile, 40-year-old female.

The surgeon wants to snatch you,
wiggle you out from the nest of innards
and extract you through a slit in my side,
but I want you to stay a while longer—
your little screeching voice,
your bilious mouth pushing out and pushing out
its stuck stones, wedged in your neck
like olive pits. You keep me in thrall
with your appetite for pain,
your possibility of rupture.

Vagina

The indignity of seeing you change,
even you. Your lips used to be springy
to the touch, a miniature trampoline,
a little fat cushion of flesh. It seems someone
let all the stuffing out. Now the inner labia,
once so tidy and trim, are stretched
and distended, and sometimes poke out
like the tip of a tongue in a cruel tease.

That's all you want me to say about you.
Lately you've grown reticent as a maiden aunt
in your middle age, desiring flannel nightgowns
and ten o'clock bedtimes. So open to proposition
in your prime, it won't be long before
you grow a white fur, prepare for hibernation.

Feet

A doctor once exclaimed, *Those are some ugly feet!*

These days you don't even look human—
nothing like a model's feet in a magazine,
slim and straight as kayaks,
squelching in the sparkly sand.
You resemble the plaster model
in the podiatrist's office, the one he uses
to demonstrate deformities.
Your bunions, knobs of throbbing bone
at the base of the big toe, have given birth
to bunionettes. Your hammer toes
are scrunched into claws, as if forever
trying to grasp at something not there.
Plantar fasciitis renders the morning's first steps
like those of the mermaid's on land,
a dance on knife points.

Still, I feel a motherly affection for you,
the runt of the litter, take you into my hands
on winter nights and rub. Caked with calluses,
studded with seed corns, you are like the old woman
on the bus who wears a purple hat
strung with birds and fruit and jingly bells—
a dropout in the race for beauty,
conformity. The years I stuffed you into stilettos
long gone, now I coddle you
with custom orthotics, sensible shoes
cosy as moccasins. Soon you'll be granted
your lifelong wish and live out the rest
of your days in Birkenstocks—
you'll be walking on air!

Birthday Party

1. Sex Doll

Her name was Envy, though there wasn't much
about her life to desire. Passed from man
to man on birthdays or other milestones, kept
for a month or a year—squashed in the back
of a closet, splayed atop a jumble of boxes
and bikes in a garage—she's seen better days.
Once a jealous wife stabbed her with a ballpoint pen;
another time someone stuck a dildo
between her legs, re-christened her Benvy.
Today she showed up on your lawn, for your 60th—
her shocked face, the O of her starving mouth,
her smooth latex skin like jailbait's.

2. Birth

Your daughter is now a mother.
She gave birth without drugs—*better*
for the baby that way—though on his exodus
into the world his shoulder snagged and the midwife
had to plunge her hand in and wrench him free.
Your daughter—brave backpacker through India,
snowboarder who shattered her collarbone—
seems stronger still, cauterised at her core,
like someone who has survived
an immolation.

3. House in the Suburbs

The irises' blue flames torch the kempt yard.
The baby's wail warbles like a siren,

scratching the pollen silence. Sunlight
through firs, slanting into the doghouse,
splashing the cedar deck. The man next to me
is minus his prostate, his wife—we mistook
her at first for a man—shorn-scalped, bald-faced,
undergoing her second bout of breast cancer.
Here we are, your friends and family—
shape-shifting in our shared stumble
towards the end. Pansies nodding,
black dog nosing for dropped berries.
Cake frilled with cream, candles guttering—
the blaze of cellophane as you unwrap
gift after gift, wiping tears
of laughter from your eyes.

Breast

Over lunch we talk about the tumour.
It has a name—*invasive mucinous carcinoma*—
and a location, time-stamped on your breast:
4:30, in the lower left quadrant.
A foreign language, but you're a quick study,
ready to navigate this strange land
you never had on your bucket list
to visit. Everyone knows a few phrases,
from friends who've made previous forays—
chemotherapy versus radiation,
the side effects of Tamoxifen,
whether soy is recommended, prohibited.
You ask the waitress for a mug
of antioxidant-rich green tea,
sacrifice the side of fries
for steamed broccoli—
it's not too late to make
the right choices, start over.

There are other things to talk about,
but we don't. Cancer beguiles us now,
so we dissect its progress
the way we once parsed
a man's every word and gesture,
puzzling his intentions—serious
or flirtatious—searching for something
sinister, some proof of deception
or faith. Later we walk out
into the January day, a glorious
blue blaze, every window of every building
on fire. The day you went to the doctor
for the results was a day like this—

No way, you thought, *no way
could there be bad news*, as though
the sun were a shield against the impossible.
So happy in your new fuzzy sweater,
looking forward to an evening alone
with your book, your cat, leftover
Christmas chocolate for dinner.
No one knows how we got this old.

Saved

Like most things, it could have been worse.
A stumble on the top step, a distracted fumble
with purse, scarf and recyclables . . .

They say nearly every fall is from the top
three steps or the bottom, and this was true for you—
once, the third from last stair transformed
into a plank of polished ice
from which you skidded and shot
into space, slamming your side
into concrete, an oceanic black bruise
blooming across your torso
like a jar of spilled ink.

This time, your body went one way
and your arm another, snatching the rail
with Olympic speed. Who knew you'd be so skilled
at saving yourself? There was a muffled pop
as tendon tore away from bone—
and then a radiant pain that raced
up and down your arm, a pain that made you curse
as you minced down the stairs to the landing
where you nearly flew, clutching the sore spot
as you ventured into the miraculous
silver sunlight, the honking street.

But you hadn't fallen. You'd saved yourself
like someone alone in the wilderness.
No indication then of the months
of agony to follow—
the daily re-tearing of the tendon
as you shrugged into a sweater,

reached for a stack of plates on the shelf,
rolled over in bed. Will it be with you
all your life, faithful, unchanged,
long after the rest of you
has grown ugly and strange?

Headache Weather

This morning you wanted the world—
buttery shoes with hot-pink soles,
armfuls of frayed lilies, a whole Black Forest cake—
and came home empty-handed,
headachy. Thirsty, fretting.
Cursed your bloated image in the mirror,
the puffy face with the piggy eyes
squinted against the light.

It was headache weather—
sickly corn syrup humidity,
bulges of bulbous grey clouds.
You gulped your pills, waited
for that sensation of expansion—
the knitted ball of pain to loosen
its angry fibres, to spread out
into a strange, still plain
of painlessness.

It's almost a loss.
The migraine knew you
better than anyone—
intimate companion, it's crawled with you
into the cave of the blackout bedroom,
shrieked inside your skull,
shredded your skin itching with codeine.

No handyman, still you spoke
its hardware language—
vice, clamp, drill, skill-saw—
its grip and grind at your temples,

its drone and wail. The nail
gun fired through your right eye.

Now opiates rush your bloodstream.
Rain mists out of the golden sky.
An invisible bird zigzags from tree
to tree, trilling its crazed song.

Aura

Little omen, little cloud on the horizon.
Shiver and shimmer in my sight-line—
electrical malfunction, lightning bolt
out of the clear sky. Shaped like a zigzag
and brighter than white, quicksilver sly,
you dart here and there in my vision field.

The countdown begins, in a shower
of platinum particles. It's part
and parcel of the migraine aura—
sounds and smells amplifying
until a sneeze, or a squirt of hand lotion,
launches the tippy boats of nausea.

Then it comes. I can hear it marching
in the distance, rolling in—
advancing army, cresting wave,
even metaphors can't keep it at bay.

I want to say, *With the force of an avalanche.*
To say, *Like staring at an eclipse.*

Dear migraine, I can see you now,
peeking at me from the far hill,
through the dark stand of trees.

Monday morning, 9 AM or so

Later we went over and over
the known details, a mantra
for your last moments on earth.
Monday morning, 9 AM or so,
your silver Audi pulled out of the garage
and paused for a moment or two
in the driveway, as if you needed
a beat of silence and solitude
before the day ahead.

I was standing at the window,
misting the sulky plants, enjoying
the banality of this suburban scene—
the neighbour heading to the office
in his suit and tie, the stay-at-home
waving from the porch in her robe and slippers—
transplanted to the downtown core,
our small rooms in the sky.

We had been neighbours for fifteen years
in the condo complex, sharing a love
for *South Park*, John Updike,
martini-fuelled conversations.
Your hand extended through the car window
in a wave hello. Or was it good-bye?
A few hours later, you were in a coma,
blood leaking into your brain in a seeping red tide.
We don't know what happened,
he was on the phone one minute,
on the floor the next . . .

The ambulance took twenty-five minutes to arrive,
twenty-five minutes during which you lost
first your voice, then the twitch in your fingertips,
then consciousness. Someone else had fallen
in the mall below your office, confusing the dispatcher—
at the same instant the aneurysm
exploded in your brain, a stranger stumbled
and smacked his head on the tile floor
five floors below, a coincidence you would have loved,
evidence of the universe's sick sense of humour.

Not that it mattered—
already your mind was erasing itself,
wiped clean like calculations from a chalkboard.
While your body, in its last moments
on earth, gave everything it had to give—
your organs passing from gloved hand
to gloved hand, pink and pulsing
and snatching from the day of your death
the chance to save four lives.

Grip

Try to put this in your poem, you said,
his hand, the way it squeezed
and squeezed the edge of his desk—

His hand,
clutching the corner of the desk
where he'd spent so many of his given hours—

As long as he held on,
he could not die.
He'd fallen to the floor
mid-sentence, phone clattering down,
the aneurysm a shooting star
that burned across his brain's firmament—

His eyes, stretched wide
with shock, pupils fixed
in their epic battle between day
and permanent night—

The teaspoon of vomit
he spat up, coffee muddled
with poached egg and oatmeal,
milky as an infant's—

His hand, grasping the edge
of his desk, polished oak
tricky as ice. As though he were swinging
above a precipice, an action hero clinging
to the side of a skyscraper, the city a chasm
yawning below—

If he could just hold on.
Then this bomb that had dropped
into the middle of his day
would be defused, and it would be time
for lunch—

What a view from this height,
the spectacular grid of his life.
Toy cars, plastic trees, ant people.
Everything he loved
about to vanish in a whoosh.

Manzanita, Oregon

The rain is changing to snow.
Endings are everywhere, these winter days—
in Manzanita we search in vain
for the photographer's studio,
duck in and out of storefronts
under hammering hail. You remember
the owner from two years ago—
the lively conversation, the oddball art,
the handmade lamp in the corner:
a gift from a friend, not for sale.

The Russian girl at the chocolate store hesitates,
spills the tragic news. *Well, basically—*
she draws a breath, sorrow fighting
with excitement—*he shot his wife
and then himself. No, no one saw it coming
they were such a sweet couple . . .*

The town must have talked
of nothing else for months. What contract is there,
what guarantee? My neighbour shaved in the shower,
tugged on socks and shoes, drove to work
one Monday morning. The last thing on his mind:
that this would be his last shower,
that he was saying good-bye to his clothes, his car,
the body he had lived in for seventy years.

At night I sit by the fire, read words by a poet
so old he glimpses the contours of the next world.
The cold air scorches my skin like ice.
Our limbs heavy with rain and mud,
the piling up of silences. Two years ago,

the tide was out at Hug Point—
you turned the corner and discovered
twin rainbows, abandoned caves,
a waterfall spilling down a cliff. We felt like explorers,
mapping a private Eden. Behind the clouds,
the sky held a vast and painful light.

Dressing for the Funeral

Sometimes this seems the saddest part,
the part you can least bear—
the laying out of black on black
against the rumpled bed, the weighing
of one lipstick against another,
creating an elegant version of yourself
the dead would not recognize.

Hairspray settles over you in a cold mist,
damps your face like dew.
These are the shortest days
before the solstice, light snipped
in mid-afternoon, the bank of charcoal cloud
clapped upon the city like a cast-iron lid.
Burnt line at the horizon.

Laundry tossing in the dryer,
furred dishes in the sink. The loneliest,
going from one small room to another
crowded with your mortal things,
yanking shoes and stockings from the chaos
in the closet, your feet treading the rutted carpet,
the heartless mirror spotted
and water-stained. Your face in it,
let's face it, soon to be a cadaver's—
the structure of bones beneath
rising a little more to the surface each year,
like a drowned corpse floating
to the lip of the lake.

The impossibility of these motions
and habits and rituals, the dead

will never again partake. The grooming,
the tidying. The thinking, too much thinking.
Then getting stuck in traffic
on the causeway, sitting and steaming
and wondering how many people have died
on their way to a funeral. Merging at last
with the metal stream of vehicles
on the open bridge, the blank vista beyond.

Summerland Redux
(with a closing line from John Updike's *Rabbit at Rest*)

Upside-down, the jet plane is a snip
of thread whiffed into the sky, a bit
of silver stitching in the ivory embroidery.
We've returned, like the geese
after the starved winter. Our older faces
in the new shaving mirror
models of disintegration—
battered landscapes pocked
and freckled with UV damage,
peppered with unplucked hairs,
splotched with blemishes.

Even the muskrat ignores us now.
Once it gathered its dinner beneath our feet
on the boardwalk, eyeing us calmly
as it continued to forage,
jaws stuffed with greens.
The reclusive beaver
has dragged a door of twigs
over the entrance to his den.

How long I've wanted to say,
This is enough.
How long I've wanted to rise
each day to the breakfast table
in the tiara of sun, in the lake's
lacquered embrace. To hike in the shadow
of the razed cliffs, tree roots clinging
to rock and air, the hush of the highway near.
Red-winged blackbirds, cinnamon teals,
the quail strutting across the street—

a backdrop of birdsong, forsythia
exploding from fenced yards
in starbursts of yellow.

Gesturing at beauty, I knock the cap
off the water bottle into the lake—
a white plastic buoy that tilts, bobs
and will outlast us, take its place
in the lace of flotsam edging the shore.
Outside our hotel, the small-town beauty queens
line up on the boardwalk for a photo opp,
silvery sashes and trailing swamp-green
gowns, their heels clunk-clunking
as they parade past, single-file.
A lollipop swirl of spilled gasoline
gleams in the protected wetlands.
Enough. Maybe. Enough.

Acknowledgements:

Some of the poems in this collection previously appeared in the following publications: *The Antigonish Review, Contemporary Verse 2, Freefall, Geist, Hong Kong International Writers Festival, Prairie Fire, Prism International, Queen's Quarterly, Ricepaper, Room, Rusty Toque* and *Vallum*.

Gratitude to the Canada Council and the BC Arts Council, for time to write. Randal Macnair at Oolichan Books, for his commitment to poetry. Ron Smith, my editor, for his careful eye and devotion to detail. John Patterson, my companion of many years, for our shared adventures near and far.

"Monday Morning, 9 am or so", "Grip", "Manzanita, Oregon" and "Dressing for the Funeral" are in memory of Rocke Robertson.

Evelyn Lau is the author of twelve books, including six previous volumes of poetry. Her prose books have been translated into a dozen languages; *Runaway: Diary of a Street Kid* was made into a CBC film. Evelyn's poetry has been chosen for the Best Canadian Poetry and Best American Poetry anthologies; her work has received the Milton Acorn People's Poetry Award, the Pat Lowther Award, a National Magazine Award, a BC Book Prize nomination and a Governor-General's nomination. Evelyn Lau served as 2011-2014 Poet Laureate for the City of Vancouver.